DRUGS

NICOTINE AND TOBACCO

A MyReportLinks.com Book

Carl R. Green

MyReportLinks.com Books

an imprint of

 Enslow Publishers, Inc. **E**

Box 398, 40 Industrial Road
Berkeley Heights, NJ 07922

This book is dedicated to my grandchildren, all of whom, I feel confident, are far too savvy to ever fall for tobacco's siren song.

MyReportLinks.com Books, an imprint of Enslow Publishers, Inc. MyReportLinks® is a registered trademark of Enslow Publishers, Inc.

Library of Congress Cataloging-in-Publication Data

Green, Carl R.
   Nicotine and tobacco / Carl R. Green.
     p. cm. — (Drugs)
   Includes bibliographical references and index.
   ISBN 0-7660-5283-4
   1. Tobacco—Health aspects—Juvenile literature. 2. Smoking—Health aspects—Juvenile literature. 3. Nicotine—Health aspects—Juvenile literature.   I. Title. II. Series: Drugs (Berkeley Heights, N.J.)
RA1242.T6G75 2005
616.86'5—dc22
                           2004018520

Printed in the United States of America

10 9 8 7 6 5 4 3 2 1

MyReportLinks.com Books
Great Books, Great Links, Great for Research!

The Internet sites listed on the next four pages can save you hours of research time. These Internet sites—we call them "Report Links"—are constantly changing, but we keep them up to date on our Web site.

Give it a try! Type http://www.myreportlinks.com into your browser, click on the series title, then the book title, and scroll down to the Report Links listed for this book.

The Report Links will bring you to great source documents, photographs, and illustrations. MyReportLinks.com Books save you time, feature Report Links that are kept up to date, and make report writing easier than ever!

Please see "To Our Readers" on the copyright page for important information about this book, the MyReportLinks.com Web site, and the Report Links that back up this book.

Please enter **DRN1962** if asked for a password.

Report Links

The Internet sites described below can be accessed at
http://www.myreportlinks.com

▶ Drugs of Abuse: Tobacco
*EDITOR'S CHOICE

Research has shown that teenagers who smoke cigarettes are much
more likely to experiment with marijuana. This Web site explores that
relationship in detail, as well as other health risks associated with
smoking cigarettes.

▶ Tobacco
*EDITOR'S CHOICE

Learn about the different types of smokeless tobacco products from this
site. You will also find a description of bidis, an even more dangerous
alternative to cigarettes.

▶ ADA Facts: Nicotine
*EDITOR'S CHOICE

Nicotine is a chemical found in cigarettes, chewing and pipe tobacco,
and cigars. It is a very addictive stimulant. This site provides you with
an overview of nicotine, including sections on its effects and risks.

▶ The Brain's Response to Nicotine
*EDITOR'S CHOICE

On this site you will find out how nicotine mimics the neurotransmitter
acetylcholine, a chemical that allows brain cells to communicate. Find out
how it also affects dopamine, another neurotransmitter.

▶ All About Smoking
*EDITOR'S CHOICE

The American Lung Association has put together a site that gives you the
facts on smoking and the dangers of secondhand smoke. Information on
how the lungs work, and examples of tobacco advertising are also included.

▶ Nicotine
*EDITOR'S CHOICE

Nicotine can cause agoraphobia (a fear of public places) and panic attacks
in teenagers. Find out about other effects at this Web site. You will also
find a link to real life stories of teenage tobacco abuse on the left-hand side
of the screen.

Report Links

The Internet sites described below can be accessed at http://www.myreportlinks.com

▶American Cancer Society

The American Cancer Society aims to "prevent cancer, save lives, and diminish suffering from cancer." Its official Web site provides helpful strategies and support for people who want to quit smoking.

▶American Lung Association

The American Lung Association works to prevent lung disease and promote lung health by providing the necessary information to the public. Check out the 'Quit Smoking' section to learn about tobacco legislation, how cigarettes affect people's lungs, and more.

▶A to Z of Drugs: Tobacco

This BBC site provides a look at tobacco, its health risks, and effects. Information is also posted on the legal problems storekeepers can get into when they sell tobacco products to minors in the United Kingdom.

▶Brief History of Tobacco Use and Abuse

Christopher Columbus was the first to bring tobacco plants and seeds to Europe. Learn about the history of tobacco in Western culture from the fifteenth century to the present day.

▶Campaign for Tobacco-Free Kids

The Campaign for Tobacco-Free Kids is an independent, non-governmental organization dedicated to fighting tobacco use among young people in the United States. Learn more about the organization at this site.

▶Cigarettes and Other Nicotine Products

The latest research on nicotine, and some of the most promising treatment approaches to quitting smoking, are discussed at this site. View the results of a survey on smoking and teenagers.

▶Citizens for Clean Air and Clean Lungs (CCAA)

Founded in 1995, the Citizens for Clean Air and Clean Lungs (CCAA) educates the public on the dangers of second-hand cigarette smoke (officially referred to as environmental tobacco smoke, ETS). Learn more about ETS and find out how you can help.

▶Girls: Lighting Up to Calm Down?

This site explains why some teenage girls start smoking. It also takes a look at two serious short-term side effects of smoking: anxiety and panic attacks.

Report Links

The Internet sites described below can be accessed at
http://www.myreportlinks.com

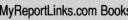

▶How Nicotine Works

This online resource provides information on what nicotine is and how it affects the body. A section on addiction and withdrawal is also included.

▶In the Know Zone: Tobacco

Find out more about the dangers of tobacco. At this Web site you will find information about the short- and long-term health effects associated with tobacco use, statistics on tobacco users, the history of tobacco use, and more.

▶Inside the Tobacco Deal

Read about the two lawyers from a small town in Mississippi whose successful lawsuit forced tobacco companies to pay for smoking-related healthcare. Their suit also changed the rules on how tobacco companies are allowed to advertise.

▶Nicotine (Tobacco)

This Neuroscience for Kids Web site contains information on how nicotine and tobacco negatively affect the nervous system.

▶NIDA: Nicotine

The National Institute on Drug Abuse Web site contains research papers, articles, and fact sheets on nicotine and tobacco use. Learn about the medical consequences of using nicotine and other drugs.

▶Preventing Tobacco Use

Tobacco control is a term used to describe programs and policies aimed at preventing or reducing tobacco use and exposure to secondhand smoke. This site shows how tobacco control saves both money and lives.

▶Questions About Smoking, Tobacco, and Health

The American Cancer Society warns of the dangers of smoking. Find information on the different kinds of tobacco products and how each affects health. Also learn how quitting pays off in almost immediate changes in the body.

▶Smoking

Get the facts on smoking tobacco from this informative Web site. Information on how using marijuana also hurts your lungs is included as well.

Report Links

The Internet sites described below can be accessed at
http://www.myreportlinks.com

▶**Smoking and Your Digestive System**

Cigarette smoking affects all parts of the body, including the digestive system. Some of the effects appear to be limited if the smoker stops while he or she is still young.

▶**Smoking Stinks**

This KidsHealth article explains the dangers and realities of smoking. It also provides some tips on how to help a friend quit smoking. Follow the 'Next Page' links on the Web site to continue reading each article.

▶**State Legislated Actions on Tobacco Issues**

Click on a state to view its tobacco use and smoking laws. You can find out how each state taxes tobacco products and the restrictions it imposes on smoking in public places. Penalties for the sale of tobacco products to youths are also included on this American Lung Association Web site.

▶**Straight Talk About Tobacco**

Tobacco-related illnesses are the leading cause of death in the United States. "Light" cigarettes and smokeless tobacco products, it turns out, are just as bad for you as any other tobacco product. Get more facts on this site, and take the quiz.

▶**The Surgeon General's Report for Kids about Smoking**

The Surgeon General is the highest-ranking doctor in the United States. This site provides information that the Surgeon General found out about smoking and young people. You can make your world smoke-free by following the nine steps listed here.

▶**TeensHealth: Smoking**

TeenHealth.com provides information on the health risks involved with smoking, as well as tips that will help teens kick the habit.

▶**Tips4Youth**

This Centers for Disease Control and Prevention Web site focuses on teenage tobacco use. Helpful information about quitting smoking and ways to avoid being tricked by tobacco advertising are included, along with interviews, tip sheets, a video, and a quiz.

▶**Tobacco.org**

Tobacco.org has current articles, news, medical reports, and tobacco-related stories from around the world. The site also has information on the history of tobacco and material on smoke-free restaurants.

NICOTINE AND TOBACCO FACTS

✘ Tobacco is made from the leaves of plants belonging to the genus *Nicotiana*.

✘ Primary uses: Cigarettes and cigars, pipe tobacco, chewing tobacco, snuff. Cigarettes account for 95 percent of tobacco use.

✘ The Tobacco Crop: Over sixty nations grow about 8.5 million tons (7.75 million metric tons) of tobacco each year.

✘ Yearly U.S. Farm Production: 820,000 tons (750,000 metric tons).

✘ Yearly U.S. Factory Production: 660 billion cigarettes, 3 billion cigars, and 140 million pounds (65 million kilograms) of smokeless tobacco products.

✘ Yearly Sales: Tobacco crop—$3 billion. Tobacco products—$25 billion.

✘ Tobacco taxes are a major source of revenue for federal, state, and local governments. Taxes per pack range from 2.5¢ in Virginia to $2.05 in New Jersey.

✘ Nicotine is an addictive alkaloid that stimulates and depresses the nervous system. In its pure form, nicotine is a powerful poison.

✘ Tobacco smoke contains hundreds of other toxins, such as carbon monoxide, sticky tars, arsenic, hydrogen cyanide, and polonium-210.

✘ Tobacco causes its most immediate damage to the lungs, heart, blood vessels, mouth, and throat.

✘ Over time, tobacco toxins can cause cancer of the lungs, throat, kidneys, and other organs. Women who smoke while pregnant may have a miscarriage or give birth to an underweight baby.

✘ Tobacco kills over 400,000 Americans each year.

✘ On average, long-term tobacco use reduces one's life span by ten years.

✘ Secondhand smoke kills up to sixty-two thousand non-smokers each year.

✘ In the United States, about 22 percent of adults use tobacco in some form.

✘ Teen Tobacco Use in Past Month:
Ages 11–13: 13 percent.
Ages 14–18: 28 percent.

✘ Cigarettes Smoked Per Person:
1900: 54. 1963: 4,345. 2002: 1,979.

A TAKE-NO-PRISONERS KILLER

As you may have noticed, life does not always make sense. If you need proof, consider this bit of evidence. The police work overtime to stamp out the use of illegal drugs such as cocaine and heroin. Although the list of addictive drugs is a long one, many people argue that it is incomplete. One highly potent drug, they say, has never made the list. Look around, and you will see large numbers of kids and adults using this drug. Whether they are smoking, chewing, or sniffing, the result is the same: Tobacco, in all its forms, is both addictive and deadly.

What makes tobacco so dangerous? Health experts say that it is the nicotine found in tobacco that causes the harm. Nicotine, they warn, is more addictive than heroin and cocaine.[1] Doctors know that nicotine is a take-no-prisoners killer. The people who use tobacco, however, seldom listen to the warnings.

How would you feel if you turned on the news tonight and heard that four giant jetliners had crashed? The death toll, the announcer says, stands at 1,200 men, women, and children. Each day, week after week, the crashes continue. By the end of the year, over 400,000 Americans have died before their time.[2]

The 400,000 deaths are real. These deaths, however, are caused by the toxins found in tobacco, not plane crashes. Year after year, the death toll mounts. Tobacco kills more people than AIDS, car and plane crashes, alcohol, homicides, fires, and illegal drug use put together. The only real difference is that tobacco kills its victims slowly. Very few teenagers die of tobacco-related causes. If these young people continue to smoke as adults, the picture

Tobacco is a dangerous drug that too many people start using while they are teenagers. It is responsible for four hundred thousand deaths a year in America alone.

changes. One third of the smokers who get hooked as teens will die of related diseases before they reach old age.[3]

Smokers Tell Their Stories

Given the risks, it is hard to understand why anyone would fool around with tobacco. Perhaps the best way to get the inside story is to talk to a few smokers. With that in mind, meet Crystal, Joshua, Liz, and Herman:*

Crystal. This high school junior makes a strong case for steering clear of cigarettes. Crystal took her first puff when she was fifteen, and quickly became addicted. "I've tried to quit several times," she says, "but here I am, still a smoker. When I don't smoke, it rips my lungs apart. When I do smoke, I feel tired and guilty." Last summer, Crystal was arrested and sentenced to six weeks of community service after she was caught stealing cigarettes. Despite that painful experience, she still smokes. "I wonder if I ever will quit," she says.[4]

Joshua. An active college student, Joshua lit up his first cigarette when he was thirteen. He knew that smoking was wrong, but he thought it would be cool to smoke with his friends. When his parents found out, "they hit the roof." Joshua promised to quit, but never did. Instead, he says, "I got real sneaky." By the time he graduated from high school, he was smoking a pack-and-a-half a day.[5]

Liz. Caught off guard by tobacco's addictive power, this athletic teenager regrets the day she took her first drag. What started out as a way to share a good time with friends soon turned sour. As a member of the school cycling team, Liz worked hard to get ready for the year's big race. Midway through the event she called on her reserves—and found that the tank was empty. With her muscles starved of oxygen, she dropped out of the race. "I've always had crazy, strong will power," Liz says, "but nicotine got the best of me. I'm fighting back, but it's no easy ride."[6]

*Disclaimer: While the stories of abuse in this book are real, many of the names have been changed.

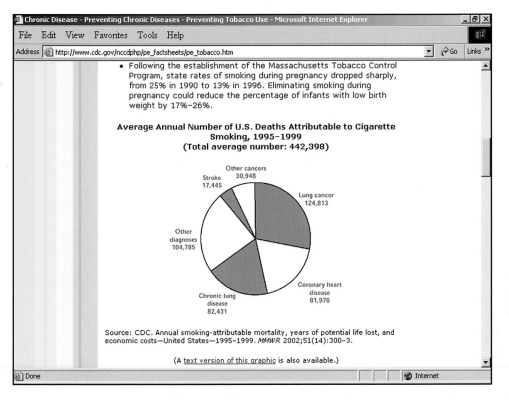

Chronic Disease - Preventing Chronic Diseases - Preventing Tobacco Use - Microsoft Internet Explorer

File   Edit   View   Favorites   Tools   Help

Address http://www.cdc.gov/nccdphp/pe_factsheets/pe_tobacco.htm   Go   Links »

- Following the establishment of the Massachusetts Tobacco Control Program, state rates of smoking during pregnancy dropped sharply, from 25% in 1990 to 13% in 1996. Eliminating smoking during pregnancy could reduce the percentage of infants with low birth weight by 17%–26%.

Average Annual Number of U.S. Deaths Attributable to Cigarette Smoking, 1995–1999
(Total average number: 442,398)

Other cancers 30,948
Stroke 17,445
Lung cancer 124,813
Other diagnoses 104,785
Coronary heart disease 81,976
Chronic lung disease 82,431

Source: CDC. Annual smoking-attributable mortality, years of potential life lost, and economic costs—United States—1995–1999. *MMWR* 2002;51(14):300–3.

(A text version of this graphic is also available.)

Done   Internet

▲ *Between the years 1995 and 1999, lung cancer was the leading cause of cigarette-related deaths, followed by chronic lung disease, coronary heart disease, and stroke.*

Herman. At age sixty-nine, Herman looks twenty years older. His face is heavily lined, and his eyes are clouded by cataracts—both the result of years of smoking. A breathing tube sticks out of the bandages wrapped around his neck. "I was only ten when my buddies and I smoked our first cigarettes," Herman says in his robot-like voice. "I've tried to stop any number of times, but I always start up again." Pausing for a moment, he pushes a cigarette into the end of his breathing tube and lights it. Moments later, smoke curls out of his nostrils. Herman winks at his visitor. "Yeah, I know how it looks," he says. "But what's a guy to do? The cancer left a hole in my throat when the surgeon took out my trachea. This is all I have left."[7]

⚠ Long-term smoking causes many internal health risks as well as affecting a person's outward appearance. This man has become wrinkled before his time, and his complexion long ago lost the healthy glow of youth.

Sooner or later, someone will offer you a chance to try tobacco. If it is not a cigarette, it might be a pipe, a cigar, a wad of chewing tobacco, or a pinch of snuff. What do you do? In your heart, you know you ought to say, "Thanks, but I don't smoke." For most of us, that is easier said than done. You do not want your friends to think you are chicken, right?

Before you say, "Sure I'll try one," think about Herman. The old man died a few weeks ago. His death certificate says he died of cancer. His wife and children know that Herman was killed by his long love affair with tobacco.

A LOVE/HATE RELATIONSHIP

Step into your shiny, new time machine. Set the controls to whisk you back to the early days of the human race. Stop when you glimpse the long-ago ancestor who first inhaled smoke from a burning leaf. Chances are this ancient cave dweller choked, gasped, and kept on breathing the fumes. In time, the practice spread. Some tribes chewed or swallowed plants prized for their medical properties. More often, these ancient peoples set fire to leaves and stems and drew the smoke into their lungs. These first

▲ Tobacco became a cash crop in the Americas soon after the first Europeans arrived. This vintage photo shows an old-time tobacco farmer readying a field for planting.

smokers probably described the mildly exhilarating effect as a gift from the gods.

Over the centuries, smokers tested any number of wild plants. As it turned out, the leafy bush destined to be the smoker's favorite grew mostly in the Americas. Experts believe it was the Mayans of Central America who first smoked tobacco leaves. From those first trials around 1000 B.C., the custom spread quickly. By the time Christopher Columbus sailed in 1492, tobacco was a highly prized crop in much of the western hemisphere.[1]

▷ The "Smoke Drinkers"

The first European explorers were baffled by the native practice of "drinking smoke." Columbus wrote in his journal, "They did wrap the tobacco in a certain leaf . . . [and] having lighted one end of it . . . they sucked, absorbed or received that smoke inside with their breath."[2] As a sign of friendship, the natives offered dried tobacco leaves to the newcomers. The sailors took a few puffs and smiled. They liked the way the smoke they inhaled from the rolled-up leaves made them feel.

A year later, tobacco was ringing alarm bells in Spain. After learning to smoke in Cuba, Rodrigo de Jerez carried his habit back to Spain. Rodrigo thought the custom was harmless, but church officials disagreed. Certain that tobacco was a tool of the devil, they threw Rodrigo into jail for three years.[3] The harsh sentence failed to stop the spread of the new practice. Shiploads of tobacco sold out as fast as the bales could be unloaded.

In 1559, Jean Nicot introduced tobacco to France. This new wonder drug, he promised, would cure cancer and other ills. To promote tobacco plantings, Nicot handed out seeds to French landowners. By 1570, the nation's doctors were rushing to treat their patients with tobacco. In his essay, "Joyful News Out of the New Found World," John Frampton described the wonders of *nicotiana*. The name, which honored Nicot, is still used. All of tobacco's many varieties belong to the genus *Nicotiana*.[4]

A Fast-growing Sensation

Almost from day one, Europeans either loved or hated tobacco. Those who fell under its spell treasured their pipes, cigars, and snuff boxes. Tobacco farmers like John Rolfe of the Virginia colony prospered by selling to this eager market. Instead of the harsh-tasting *Nicotiana rustica,* Rolfe and his wife, Pocahontas, grew a milder Spanish variety. Despite Spain's attempts to guard their stocks of *Nicotiana tabacum,* Rolfe was able to obtain seeds from Trinidad. He sent his first shipload to London in 1614, where it sold out quickly. By 1622, England and Ireland were buying all the tobacco Virginia's farmers could grow.

Each country developed its own ways of using tobacco. Wealthy American colonists smoked cigars. Farmers and workmen stuck "chaws" of chewing tobacco into their cheeks. Spittoons became standard fixtures in homes, workshops, and taverns. In England, Sir Walter Raleigh

This man is cutting tobacco leaves for harvest.

▲ *James Duke was the first to mass produce cigarettes. His use of rolling machines created cigarettes as we know them today.*

inspired an era of pipe smoking. When the common people took up the pipe, British gentlemen switched to snuff. The sneezes triggered by a pinch of snuff were said to clear the head and brighten the eyes. In Spain, cigars reigned as the favorite smoke until the mid-1800s. The custom changed when soldiers picked up the Turkish habit of smoking tiny tobacco sticks wrapped in thin papers. The custom gave birth to the best-selling smoke of all—the cigarette.[5]

In 1881, cigarettes made up only one percent of American tobacco sales. Chewing tobacco was king, followed by pipes and cigars. Often called coffin nails or Satan sticks, cigarettes drew little but scorn. All that changed when James Duke came along. The North Carolina native gambled that the cigarette could save his family's failing tobacco business. Duke started by finding better ways to cure and blend his tobaccos. Next, he replaced skilled hand-rollers with cigarette-making machines. With each machine doing the work of forty-eight hand-rollers, Duke was able to cut prices. Within a few years, his company's sales had topped a billion packs a year.[6]

Rise of the Anti-smoking Movement

By the late 1880s, tobacco sales were booming. Famous people, from actors to presidents, could be seen smoking in public. Alarmed by the tobacco frenzy, *The New York Times* cautioned that cigarettes would be "the ruin of the Republic."[7] As more and more voices echoed those warnings, the anti-smoking movement was born.

Lucy Page Gaston founded the Anti-Cigarette League (ACL) in 1899. Her message was simple: Outlaw the production and sale of cigarettes. Powerful factory owners like Andrew Carnegie and Henry Ford joined in the crusade. Ford took the lead by refusing to hire cigarette smokers for his auto plant. ACL members urged schoolchildren to sign non-smoking pledges. Eleven states joined in by passing laws that banned the sale of cigarettes. From that high point, the movement soon faltered. Out on the streets, the police often looked the other way as bootleggers sold smuggled cigarettes. Cigarette companies sidestepped the laws by "giving" their products away—and charging for the matches.[8]

Tobacco users put an end to the fuss by refusing to give up their smokes and chews. Only in the past fifty years, after tobacco's health hazards were proven, has the tide turned. Once started, the breakthroughs came quickly. Here are some major turning points:

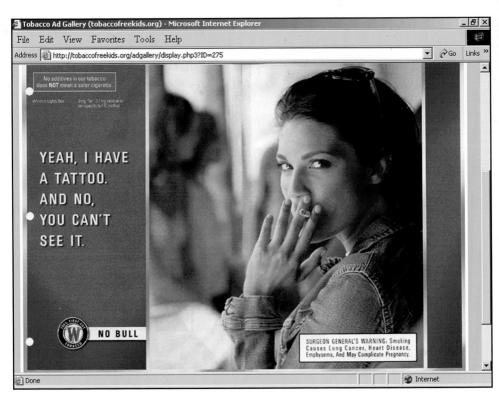

File   Edit   View   Favorites   Tools   Help

Address http://tobaccofreekids.org/adgallery/display.php3?ID=275

No additives in our tobacco
does **NOT** mean a safer cigarette.

Winston Lights Box   3mg "tar", 0.7mg nicotine av.
                          per cigarette by FTC method

YEAH, I HAVE
A TATTOO.
AND NO,
YOU CAN'T
SEE IT.

NO BULL

SURGEON GENERAL'S WARNING: Smoking
Causes Lung Cancer, Heart Disease,
Emphysema, And May Complicate Pregnancy.

▲ *The tobacco industry spends over $12.4 billion per year on marketing its products. This amounts almost to $34 million per day. Many tobacco advertisements, such as this one, try to make smoking appear attractive and cool.*

1952—*Reader's Digest* reports that cigarette smoking is linked to lung cancer.

1964—The U.S. Surgeon General issues a stern warning about the health hazards of smoking. After a brief slump, tobacco sales bounce back.

1966—Congress orders tobacco companies to print warning labels on cigarette packs. The first label reads, *Caution: Cigarette Smoking May Be Hazardous to Your Health.*

1969—A new federal law bans cigarette ads on television and radio. The warning label now reads, *Warning: The Surgeon General Has Determined That Cigarette Smoking Is Dangerous to Your Health.* In 1981, the warnings are further strengthened.

1975—Minnesota passes a law that allows smoking only in posted areas. The drive to protect the right of nonsmokers to breathe clean air spreads quickly.

1986—The Surgeon General warns that secondhand smoke is hazardous to nonsmokers. The tobacco companies protest the posting of no-smoking signs, but to little avail. Humorist Dave Barry observes, "Today, lighting a cigarette in a restaurant is about as socially acceptable as wandering around spitting into people's salads."[9]

1997—Big Tobacco's winning streak in the courts ends in a massive defeat. With their backs to the wall, tobacco companies agree to pay $368.5 billion to cover the medical costs of cigarette-related illnesses. A year later, the companies sign off on another $206 billion payout to the states.[10]

Today, non-smoking zones have spread to schools, restaurants, bars, offices, stores, and even beaches. Despite their long series of setbacks, the tobacco companies still market their products as safe and sexy. A close look at what smokers are inhaling tells a far different story.

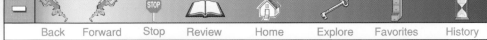
STOREHOUSE OF TOXINS

At first glance, tobacco, in any form, looks quite harmless. Besides, it is legal to sell tobacco products, right? So, how can such widely used products pose such a threat?

Tobacco, lab reports warn, is packed with over four thousand harmful chemicals. Chemists label these compounds as toxins—a polite name for poisons. Nicotine, the chief villain, is a highly toxic poison. Eight drops of pure nicotine will kill a horse in four minutes. One drop placed on the tongue will kill a human being. Smokers would die quick, painful deaths if their bodies allowed nicotine to build up in the tissues.[1]

Tobacco's toxic effects do not end with nicotine. Along with providing sticky tars to clog the lungs, a cigarette delivers another four thousand chemicals. Sixty-nine of them are known to cause cancer in mammals, forty of them cause cancer in humans.[2] Like asbestos and benzene, tobacco smoke is ranked as a cancer-causing Group A carcinogen. If tobacco's "ingredients" were printed on the pack, the list would include:

◁ *Tobacco is loaded with toxins and other poisons. There are over four thousand harmful chemicals in tobacco, and sixty-nine of them can cause cancer.*

Arsenic—A deadly rat poison. Causes a numb "pins and needles" feeling in the arms and feet.

Acetone—A chemical often used in paint thinner.

Benzene—A solvent often used in rubber cement.

Butane—Can be used as a fuel.

Cadmium—Found in artists' oil paints. Leaves yellow stains on teeth.

Carbon monoxide—A toxic gas found in car exhaust fumes.

Formaldehyde—A chemical used to preserve dead bodies.

Hydrogen cyanide—A poison used in gas chambers.

Napthalenes—Used in explosives, moth balls, and paint. Causes headaches and confusion.

Polonium-210—A highly radioactive element.[3]

Toluene—A chemical used to make embalmer's glue.

Vinyl chloride—A chemical used to make garbage bags.

The list of toxins helps explain this off-the-cuff remark by a tobacco company official. Asked why he did not smoke the cigarettes he sold, the man laughed. "We don't smoke the [stuff]," he said. "We just sell it. We reserve [smoking] for the young, the poor, . . . and the stupid."[4]

▷ Smokers Put Their Health at Risk

You do not have to be young, poor, or stupid to put your health at risk. Anyone who smokes tobacco, chews it, or uses snuff is betting against the odds. Doctors pin the blame on the action of nicotine and other toxins on the body. Some of the health effects appear almost at once. Others take years to develop. Nicotine does its part by getting to work in a flash. Take a drag on a cigarette, and the brain receives a nicotine jolt eight seconds later. Heroin takes twice as long to reach the brain.[5]

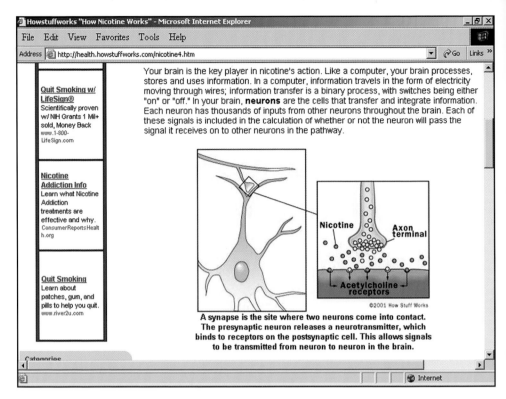

Howstuffworks "How Nicotine Works" - Microsoft Internet Explorer

File   Edit   View   Favorites   Tools   Help

Address   http://health.howstuffworks.com/nicotine4.htm   Go   Links »

**Quit Smoking w/
LifeSign®**
Scientifically proven
w/ NIH Grants 1 Mil+
sold, Money Back
www.1-800-
LifeSign.com

**Nicotine
Addiction Info**
Learn what Nicotine
Addiction
treatments are
effective and why.
ConsumerReportsHealt
h.org

Quit Smoking
Learn about
patches, gum, and
pills to help you quit.
www.river2u.com

Categories

Your brain is the key player in nicotine's action. Like a computer, your brain processes, stores and uses information. In a computer, information travels in the form of electricity moving through wires; information transfer is a binary process, with switches being either "on" or "off." In your brain, **neurons** are the cells that transfer and integrate information. Each neuron has thousands of inputs from other neurons throughout the brain. Each of these signals is included in the calculation of whether or not the neuron will pass the signal it receives on to other neurons in the pathway.

Nicotine   Axon terminal   Acetylcholine receptors   ©2001 How Stuff Works

A synapse is the site where two neurons come into contact. The presynaptic neuron releases a neurotransmitter, which binds to receptors on the postsynaptic cell. This allows signals to be transmitted from neuron to neuron in the brain.

Once it reaches the brain, nicotine acts as a neurotransmitter, causing the body to feel reenergized and happy. Because nicotine also strengthens your body's memory of these good feelings, it boosts your desire for another smoke, chaw, or sniff.

Tobacco's bouquet of toxins triggers a long-lasting chain reaction. Most of all, users treasure the quick nicotine rush. Most people say they soon feel relaxed and alert. Nicotine and the other toxins also temporarily suppress hunger and seem to sharpen the memory. A smoker who feels angry, tense, or bored gets a quick lift. This mood-changing effect would hook many people, even without nicotine's other addictive powers. In time, the smoker links these mood changes with having a good time. Smoking becomes a vital part of activities such as partying or unwinding after a tough day.

Tobacco's health effects show up first in the mouth. Along with bad breath, smokers can look forward to stained teeth, gum disease, and tooth loss. The lungs pay an even higher price. Many users develop heavy coughs and are more likely to catch the flu. Athletes report that smoking robs them of breath and endurance. With tar clogging the lungs, the heart and other muscles do not receive enough oxygen. The bottom line is quite clear: You can smoke or you can compete in sports. You cannot do both with any great success.

Despite these dangers, people still use tobacco. Over the years, the habit becomes more difficult to break and the risk of illness increases sharply. A British study puts the risk in sharp focus. For fifty years, researchers have followed a group of doctors, all of them lifelong smokers. The bottom line, says Richard Doll, is that smoking cuts ten years off one's life. Think of it this way: A seventy-year-old non-smoker has a 33 percent chance of living to age ninety. A seventy-year-old smoker has only a 7 percent chance of living another twenty years.[6]

Can I Smoke Now and Quit Later?

Screenwriter Joe Eszterhas admits to a lifelong addiction to tobacco. For years, he smoked up to four packs of cigarettes a day. In films like *Flashdance,* he wrote scenes that made smoking look both sexy and cool. The romance came to a sudden halt the day his doctor told him he had throat cancer. Quitting, Eszterhas says, was the toughest thing he had ever done. At one point, wracked by a fierce urge to smoke, he sat down on a curb and cried. After that low point, he slowly took charge of his life. Now, like many ex-smokers, Eszterhas works hard at getting out the anti-smoking message.[7]

The Surgeon General's Report of 1988 spelled out the dangers. "Nicotine dependency is . . . the most common form of drug addiction," the report says. It is also "the one that causes more death and disease than all other addictions combined."[8] The road to addiction is posted with these warning signs:

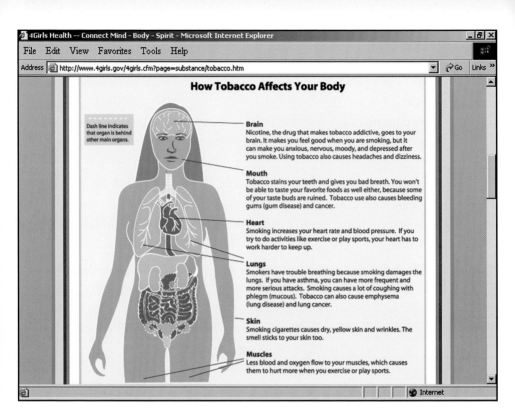

▲ Smoking cigarettes is not worth the damage the addiction inflicts on your body.

- Smoking, chewing, or dipping ever greater quantities of tobacco.
- Craving tobacco and not being able to quit.
- Trying to quit triggers withdrawal symptoms such as headaches, anxiety, and bad temper.
- Continuing to use tobacco despite knowing how harmful it is.[9]

How strong is this addiction? A researcher asked former alcoholics and other drug addicts that question. Two thirds of the drinkers said their craving for tobacco was stronger than their craving for alcohol. Among addicts, one in five rated the urge to smoke as strong or stronger than the need for heroin.[10] Brain scans have revealed the source of this powerful addiction. A jolt of nicotine, the scans show, heads straight to the brain's reward center. The brain responds with the message, "That felt good! Do it again."[11]

A patient under treatment for a lung ailment knew that feeling all too well. Asked her thoughts about quitting, she said she could not give up her cigarettes. "Smoking is my . . . best friend," she explained. The words must have stunned her doctors. The woman's "best friend," they knew, was killing her.[12]

Do Health Warnings Do Their Job?

The health warnings found on cigarette packages and in tobacco ads spell out the dangers. By law, each pack and each ad must include one of these four labels:

Surgeon General's Warning: Smoking Causes Lung Cancer, Heart Disease, Emphysema, and May Complicate Pregnancy.

Surgeon General's Warning: Quitting Smoking Now Greatly Reduces Serious Risk to Your Health.

Surgeon General's Warning: Smoking by Pregnant Women May Result in Fetal Injury, Premature Birth, and Low Birth Weight.

More tenth grade girls are smoking today than are their male classmates—17 percent to 16.2 percent. Those girls who became addicted to tobacco will someday run the risk of causing severe damage to their unborn babies when they become pregnant.

Many local and state governments are trying to reduce the risk of secondhand smoke to nonsmokers. New York City, for example, has banned smoking in all public places.

Surgeon General's Warning: Cigarette Smoke Contains Carbon Monoxide.[13]

Health experts worry that smokers seldom read the warnings. If they had their way, they would put large caution signs on each pack. "Do it like Canada does," they urge. The warnings on Canadian cigarette packs cover half of the front and half of the back. On a typical pack, full-color photos show the effect of smoking-related cancer on the mouth. Large type spells out a blunt warning: "Cigarettes Cause Mouth Diseases." In a survey, 44 percent of the smokers polled said the warnings increased their desire to quit.[14]

Non-smokers applaud any attempt to reduce smoking. Along with saving the lives of others, they want to safeguard their own health. One government study blames secondhand smoke for killing between thirty-five thousand and sixty-two thousand non-smokers each year. The three biggest killers are heart disease, lung cancer, and SIDS (sudden infant death syndrome).[15] That is one of the reasons some California beaches now display "No Smoking" signs. In 2003, New York City went a step further by banning smoking in all public places. The anti-tobacco movement is gaining strength, but Big Tobacco still has some tricks up its sleeve.

Chapter 4

SELLING A LEGAL (AND PROFITABLE) DRUG

Tobacco manufacturers know that many older smokers will die early, painful deaths. Tobacco's future, therefore, lies in hooking young people early. Studies show that less than 10 percent of new smokers pick up their habit after they turn twenty.[1] In pursuit of that market, tobacco officials often say one thing and mean another. R. J. Reynolds, for example, says it is shocked to think that kids might use its products:

"R. J. Reynolds Tobacco Company does not want children to smoke, not only because it is illegal in every state, but also because of the

Throughout the twentieth century, tobacco companies knowingly marketed their products to young people, even after the federal government outlawed the sale of tobacco products to anyone under the age of eighteen.

inherent health risks of smoking and because children lack the
. . . judgment to assess those risks."[2]

So, is R. J. Reynolds doing all it can to discourage teen smoking? Ask yourself that question after you read this company memo:

"To ensure increased and longer-term growth for CAMEL
FILTER, the brand must increase its share penetration
among the 14–24 age group . . . which represent tomorrow's
cigarette business."[3]

Clearly, the big tobacco manufacturers have their eye on
young people. The long road to their hearts begins on the farms
that grow *Nicotiana tabacum.*

Growing and Pricing Tobacco Crops

Tobacco got its start in the western hemisphere, but it now grows
in over sixty countries. China is the leading producer. The United
States ranks as the second-largest grower, followed by Brazil,
India, and Turkey. More than half of the United States tobacco
crop is grown in North Carolina and Kentucky. Add in the other
fourteen tobacco states, and the yearly crop weighs in at 820,000
tons (750,000 metric tons).[4]

By any measure, tobacco is big business. American tobacco
farmers harvest crops worth about $3 billion a year. Big Tobacco's
factories turn the dried leaves into some 660 billion cigarettes and
3 billion cigars a year. The rest of the crop goes into pipe tobacco,
chewing tobacco, and snuff. Buying these products costs con-
sumers about $25 billion a year.[5]

Anti-tobacco groups want tobacco farmers to switch to other
crops. The farmers cling to their way of life, aided by a government support program. Each year, the Department of Agriculture
guarantees tobacco farmers a fair market price. In return, the
farmers limit their plantings. When tobacco companies try to
switch to cheap foreign tobacco, the government does its best to
limit imports.[6]

Tobacco companies spend over a billion dollars a year on advertising. Their ads show images of sexy men and women hard at work or having fun. The truth is that smoking can hurt a person's ability to enjoy physical activities.

Marketing Tobacco Products

How does Big Tobacco sell 33 billion packs of cigarettes a year? Starting in the 1880s, the cigarette companies lured buyers with catchy names and fancy labels. Ads popped up on billboards, store counters, and even the sides of barns. Some brands offered coupons worth half a cent each. In 1913, a brand called Camels took a new tack. Splashy ads urged smokers to switch to Camels' "secret blend of Turkish and domestic tobaccos." The strategy paid off. Six years later, Camels ruled the United States cigarette market.[7]

By the 1920s, smoking had become a national passion. In a 1926 magazine ad, a young woman coos to her cigarette-smoking date, "Blow some my way." Radio commercials helped turn Lucky Strike into a best-selling brand. Later, when television came along, tobacco marketers lined up to sponsor hit shows. Big Tobacco also sponsored tennis tournaments and auto races. On college campuses, sales reps handed out free cigarettes. Teachers passed out free book covers ablaze with brand logos.

The marketing rush began to slow in 1969. First, tobacco ads were removed from the airwaves. Then, in the 1990s, Big Tobacco agreed to further limits, such as a ban on clothing with brand logos. Popular cartoon figures also bit the dust. Joe Camel vanished after research showed that he was selling kids on the idea that smoking was harmless and fun.[8] Despite these setbacks, tobacco companies found ways to pour 11 billion dollars into marketing their products in 2001.[9]

▲ It is important for parents and older siblings to warn young people about the dangers of smoking. Many school kids try their first cigarettes when they are barely into their teens.

The anti-smoking campaign is still winning victories. Today's film and television actors seldom light up on screen. More and more public places have posted no-smoking signs. Almost everyone agrees that smoking is bad for one's health. Somehow, that hard truth seems to have escaped the notice of one segment of society—young, wannabe smokers.

Why Do Kids Start Smoking?

The chances are good that you know someone who uses tobacco. Twelve percent of American fifteen-year-olds smoke every day.[10] Talk to some of them, and you will hear the same stories over and over again.

Some young smokers say they just want to see what it feels like to puff on a cigarette. In their minds, smoking makes them feel "grown up." Other teens smoke because their parents smoke or as an act of rebellion against their parents. Just as often, they blame peer pressure. If your friends are smoking, it is hard to walk away. Boys like to think that smoking makes them look like a Marlboro cowboy. Girls sometimes smoke because they hope it will help them lose weight.[11] Both sexes have the false hope that smoking makes them look cool and sexy.

Many first-time smokers fall in love with nicotine's side effects. Cigarettes give them an energy boost, they say, and help them relax. At parties or while "hanging out," holding a cigarette gives them something to do with their hands. Young people who feel stressed out use a cigarette or a chaw of tobacco to help them relax. Teens who suffer from depression find temporary relief in nicotine's stimulating high.[12]

Five Steps to a Nicotine Addiction

Research shows that young smokers follow a five-step path. The further one goes down the path, the harder it is to stop. Here is the road map:

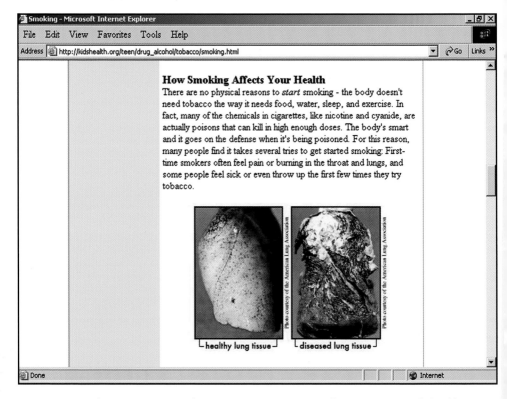

How Smoking Affects Your Health

There are no physical reasons to *start* smoking - the body doesn't need tobacco the way it needs food, water, sleep, and exercise. In fact, many of the chemicals in cigarettes, like nicotine and cyanide, are actually poisons that can kill in high enough doses. The body's smart and it goes on the defense when it's being poisoned. For this reason, many people find it takes several tries to get started smoking: First-time smokers often feel pain or burning in the throat and lungs, and some people feel sick or even throw up the first few times they try tobacco.

⌐healthy lung tissue⌐   ⌐diseased lung tissue⌐

Photo courtesy of the American Lung Association

🔘 Done   🌐 Internet

▲ Smoking poisons your lungs over time. It eventually turns a normal, healthy lung (left) into a sac of scarred, diseased tissue.

Stage 1: *Preparation.* Some teens feel that smoking is a social, adult thing to do. Others shy away, scared off by the costs, in money and in health risks. A third group views tobacco with mixed feelings. Keith, a high school freshman, tells himself, "Sure, smoking sometimes causes cancer in old people. But, hey, why worry about something that may never happen to me?"

Stage 2: *First Tries.* The day comes when Keith sets his fears and his parents' warnings aside. Egged on by his friends, he tries a few cigarettes. Very likely, the first drags make him cough and leave him feeling dizzy. Now Keith stands at a crossroads—he can turn the next smoke down or he can move on to stage three.

Stage 3: *Experimenting.* In stage three, Keith lights up only at "special" times. "I can take cigarettes or leave them alone," he claims. During soccer season, he lays off completely, convinced that smoking and sports do not mix. Then, at a party after the last game, he celebrates by smoking three "cigs" in a row. "I needed that," he says with a smile.

Stage 4: *Regular Use.* By the time he reaches his junior year, Keith has moved into stage four. When he feels stressed out, or while relaxing with his buddies, he pulls out a cigarette. He knows a shop that sells to minors, and his older brother slips him a pack now and then. Sometimes he quits for a few days, just to prove he can. When he does, the need for a smoke grows stronger with each passing hour.

Stage 5: *Addiction.* One or two cigarettes no longer satisfy Keith's craving for nicotine. Asked about his pack-a-day smoking, he shrugs. "I'll quit when I'm older," he says. Keith is well down the road to becoming a lifetime smoker.[13]

As far back as the 1970s, President Jimmy Carter objected to the way Big Tobacco markets its products. We must do a better job of protecting our young people, he said. "If the tobacco companies win," he warned, "our children lose."[14]

Chapter 5

WINNING THE TOBACCO WARS

Check out the fresh faces in any middle school classroom. Of the thirty-two kids sitting there, four have used tobacco in the past thirty days. Now, hop over to the high school. Nine members of this first-period math class smoked, chewed, or dipped tobacco last month.[1] Some will make up their minds to quit, and mean it. All too soon, others will need a nicotine "fix" to get through each day. Of this number, at least half will go on to smoke for twenty years or more.[2]

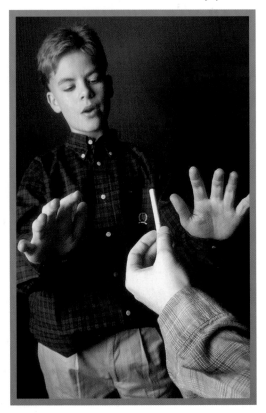

Teen smokers often think their youth and good health will shield them from tobacco's ill effects. If so, they should study the data. Bad breath and stained teeth are just the start. Young people who smoke have a much greater chance of developing asthma and chronic bronchitis than do nonsmokers. Smokers also tend to have lower self-esteem, poorer grades, more colds, and higher rates of

◀ Sometimes all it takes is a handful of cigarettes to get hooked on nicotine and tobacco. It is important to simply decline the offer when someone tries to talk you into trying your first cigarette.

depression. Even the ones that are good students are more likely to drop out of school.[3]

Sue, a high school junior and budding artist, was one of those who got the message. "Like a lot of my friends, I smoked for a while—grape-flavored bidis from India, mostly. I remember feeling way cool, a real rebel." Sue smiles and smacks herself on the head. "Before long I was craving three or four smokes a day. So, I quit, just like that. Now, when someone offers me a smoke, I say, 'Thanks, but no thanks.'"

Here Is the Scoop on How to Say "No"

Sue was lucky. Most people cannot quit that easily. The easiest way to deal with tobacco is to never take that first drag or chaw. With a little practice, you can learn to say "No" without sounding like a geek. When you find yourself in a tough spot, rely on the five knows:

Know yourself. Think about what you believe, who you are, and who you want to be. When pushed to make a tough choice, listen to that clear inner voice that knows what is right and wrong for you.

Know the facts. It helps to know the enemy. It is a fact, for example, that tobacco is both addictive and expensive. In some states, teenagers can lose their driver's license if they are caught smoking.

Know the situation. Be alert to clues that tell you trouble is brewing. Are your friends saying, "Don't be chicken!" or "No one will know"? Question their motives. They may be trying to justify their own use by getting you involved.

Know how to avoid trouble. There are lots of ways to say "No." Try using humor, or come up with a better plan for having fun. Deflect bad feelings by saying, "You're too smart (or too cool) to do that!"

Know how to get help. Everyone needs help now and then. When your time comes, turn to a trusted adult. This might be a parent, pastor, teacher, counselor, or relative. Asking for help is a sign of strength.[4]

Every day, some two thousand kids light up for the first time. Five cigarettes later, many of them will have started down the road to addiction. And sooner or later, they will wish they could quit the habit.

Kicking the Nicotine Habit

Asked to explain the addictive nature of his habit, Sam has a ready answer. "Addiction is needing to smoke first thing in the morning, not just when you are bored or hanging out with your friends," the teenager says.[5] Sam can tell you how hard it was to break tobacco's hold on his body. Along with feeling tense and ill-tempered, he felt dizzy and headachy. His hands trembled, and he had trouble sleeping. "I was hungry all the time," Sam says. "I must have put on ten pounds that first month." The symptoms have eased, but six months later his craving for tobacco is still strong.[6]

Smokers, young and old, can, and do, win this battle. If, like Sam,

Kicking a nicotine habit can take time, but there are many organizations that offer help.

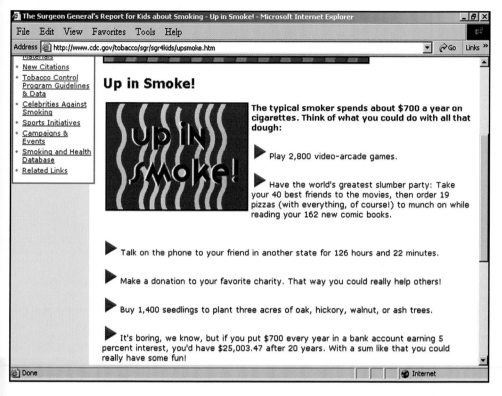

The Surgeon General's Report for Kids about Smoking - Up in Smoke! - Microsoft Internet Explorer

File   Edit   View   Favorites   Tools   Help

Address http://www.cdc.gov/tobacco/sgr/sgr4kids/upsmoke.htm   Go   Links »

* New Citations
* Tobacco Control Program Guidelines & Data
* Celebrities Against Smoking
* Sports Initiatives
* Campaigns & Events
* Smoking and Health Database
* Related Links

Up in Smoke!

The typical smoker spends about $700 a year on cigarettes. Think of what you could do with all that dough:

▶ Play 2,800 video-arcade games.

▶ Have the world's greatest slumber party: Take your 40 best friends to the movies, then order 19 pizzas (with everything, of course!) to munch on while reading your 162 new comic books.

▶ Talk on the phone to your friend in another state for 126 hours and 22 minutes.

▶ Make a donation to your favorite charity. That way you could really help others!

▶ Buy 1,400 seedlings to plant three acres of oak, hickory, walnut, or ash trees.

▶ It's boring, we know, but if you put $700 every year in a bank account earning 5 percent interest, you'd have $25,003.47 after 20 years. With a sum like that you could really have some fun!

Done   Internet

▲ Smoking is a very expensive habit. The average smoker spends seven hundred dollars each year on cigarettes. What could you do with that much money?

you are fighting a nicotine habit, these steps will help you regain control:

Step 1: *Preparing to quit.* Write down the reasons you want to quit. Keep the list with you at all times. Tell some non-smoking friends and family members about your vow. Ask them to back you up when the going gets tough. Stock up on gum, sugarless candy, and flavored toothpicks. Stick something in your mouth when you feel the urge to smoke. Make a list of the rewards you will earn for staying smoke free. Give yourself a payoff after a day, a week, a month, and so on. Pay for your treats with the cash you save by not buying tobacco.

Step Two: *Taking the plunge.* Ask a doctor to recommend a temporary nicotine replacement product that gradually weans you off nicotine. Nicotine patches, sprays, and other products can double your chances of winning the battle. Get rid of everything that reminds you of tobacco—half-empty packs, matches, ashtrays, pipes, and so on. When the big day comes, quit cold turkey. Trying to "taper off," or quit by slowly reducing the amount you smoke in a week or a day, seldom works. The caffeine in coffee, tea, and soft drinks will add to your jitters. Flush the nicotine out of your system by drinking lots of juice and water. Steer clear of other smokers. If people do light up, ask them not to smoke while you are around. Leave if someone ignores your plea. When the urge to smoke kicks in, take deep, relaxing breaths. As you do so, repeat this mantra: *The urge will pass, whether or not I smoke.* The craving usually slacks off in five or ten minutes. It also helps to eat a diet that is high in protein and very low in sugar. This will help you avoid mood swings that could bring back the urge to smoke.

Step Three: *Finding help.* Remember, you have allies in this war. When the going gets tough, call on the family members, friends, or counselors you lined up earlier. If you cannot reach your allies, help is just a mouse click or a phone call away. Look in the back of this book for helpful phone numbers. Join a "kick butts" program geared to people like you. Check your local hospitals and clinics for workshops, or ask your school counselor to help you find one.[7]

What Comes Next?

Year after year, tobacco kills over 400,000 of its best customers. To spotlight that hard, sad fact, a team of anti-smokers formed a make-believe company called Licensed to Kill, Inc. The founders claim that L2K, their "flagship brand," delivers what all smokers

▲ Smoking is a habit that can hurt your appearance, leave you short of breath, and eventually kill you. If it makes this ashtray look this nasty, think about what it could do to your lungs and body.

want: heavy doses of tar, nicotine, and toxic chemicals. With a knowing wink, the L2K Web site explains, "People pay us to kill them. That is why our motto is 'We're Rich. You're Dead.'"[8]

L2K hopes its dark humor will make you think twice about embracing this deadly killer. The real joke, remember, is on anyone who uses tobacco products. Is the "hit" the smoker gets when nicotine reaches the brain worth the risk of dying young?

The choice is up to you. Make it a good one!

addiction—Involuntary psychological, physical, or emotional dependence upon a substance that is known by the user to be harmful.

bidis—Small, flavored cigarettes usually made in India. Bidis contain more tar and nicotine than regular cigarettes.

bootlegger—Someone who makes or sells alcohol illegally.

carcinogen—A toxic substance or agent that can cause cancer.

chew—Chewing tobacco that the user places between the gums and the cheek. Also called chaw and dip.

dipping—Using chewing tobacco.

drag—A slow inhalation of smoke.

emphysema—A permanent lung disease (commonly caused by long-term smoking) in which enlarged air sacs block the flow of air into the lungs.

intoxicate—To bring about a state of mind ranging from exhilaration to stupefaction through the use of drugs or alcohol.

snuff—Finely powdered tobacco that is most often inhaled. Snuff can also be chewed or placed between the gums and the cheek.

spittoon—A bowl-shaped container that tobacco chewers use when they need to spit.

Surgeon General—As head of the United States Public Health Service, the surgeon general ranks as the nation's chief medical officer.

withdrawal—A syndrome of often painful physical and psychological symptoms that an addict suffers when trying to kick his or her drug habit.

Chapter Notes

Chapter 1. A Take-No-Prisoners Killer

1. CBS 2, "Nicotine Is More Addictive Than Heroin," *Action on Smoking and Health,* March 28, 2001, <http://www.no-smoking.org/march01/03-28-01-2.html> (December 28, 2004).

2. Robert Schwebel, *Keep Your Kids Tobacco-Free* (New York: Newmarket Press, 2001), p. 5.

3. Ibid.

4. Marc Perkel, "Letters From Teenagers About Smoking," n.d., <http://www.perkel.com/politics/issues/smokelet.htm> (December 27, 2004).

5. Schwebel, pp. 1–3.

6. "What's Wrong with Nicotine," *Discover Films Video,* n.d., <http://www.discover-films.com/wwwn.html> (February 13, 2004).

7. Bob Beale, "Flaming Turkey," *Bulletin EdDesk Article,* n.d., <http://bulletin.ninemsn.com.au/bulletin/EdDesk.nsf/0/c88cc7168 c1fdf59ca256a1d00183cea?OpenDocument> (June 22, 2004).

Chapter 2. A Love/Hate Relationship

1. "The History of Smoking," *Forest on Line,* February 1, 2003, <http://www.forestonline.org/output/page34.asp> (June 25, 2004).

2. Arlene B. Hirschfelder, *Encyclopedia of Smoking and Tobacco* (Phoenix, Ariz.: Oryx Press, 1999), p. 89.

3. "The History of Smoking."

4. "Brief History of Tobacco Use and Abuse," *Walter Reed Army Medical Center,* February 10, 1998, <http://www.wrame.amedd .army.mil/education/tobaccohistory.htm> (June 25, 2004).

5. Ibid.

6. Cassandra Tate, *Cigarette Wars: the Triumph of "The Little White Slaver"* (New York: Oxford University Press, 1999), pp. 11–16.

7. Ibid.

8. Hirschfelder, pp. 17–18.

9. Dave Barry, "Ashes to Ashes," *totse.com,* n.d., <http://www.totse.com/en/ego/literary_genius/ashes.html> (December 27, 2004).

10. Hirschfelder, pp. 309–310.

Chapter 3. Storehouse of Toxins

1. Arlene B. Hirschfelder, *Encyclopedia of Smoking and Tobacco* (Phoenix, Ariz.: Oryx Press, 1999), p. 224.

2. Ontario Campaign for Action on Tobacco, "Second-Hand Smoke," n.d., <http://www.ocat.org/healtheffects/> (December 29, 2004).

3. "What's Really in a Cigarette?" *Kick Butts Day,* February 12, 2003, <http://kickbuttsday.org/activities/2004/WhatsReallyInaCigarette.pdf> (July 5, 2004).

4. "Test Your Tobacco IQ," *Joe Chemo,* n.d., <http://www.joechemo.org/cgi-bin/iq.cgi> (February 4, 2004).

5. William Everett Bailey, *The Invisible Drug* (Houston: Mosaic Publications, 1996), p. 87.

6. Marc Kaufman, "Cigarettes Cut About 10 Years Off Life," *Action on Smoking and Health,* June 23, 2004, <http://non-smoking.org/june04/06-23-04-5.html> (June 28, 2004).

7. Joe Eszterhas, et al, "Smoking: Join Joe to Quit Now," *WebMD,* November 20, 2003, <http://my.webmd.com/content/article/77/95433.htm> (June 22, 2004).

8. "1988 Surgeon General Report: The Health Consequences of Smoking," *Center for Disease Control,* n.d., <http://www.cdc.gov/tobacco/sgr/sgr_1988/1988SGR-Intro.pdf> (December 28, 2004).

9. Ibid.

10. David Krogh, *Smoking: the Artificial Passion* (New York: W. H. Freeman and Co., 1991), p. 94.

11. Bailey, p. 78.

12. Ibid., p. 80.

13. "Warning Label Fact Sheet," Center for Disease Control, n.d., <http://www.cdc.gov/tobacco/sgr/sgr_2000/factsheets/factsheet_labels.htm> (July 5, 2004).

14. "Canada Study: Graphic Cigarette Warnings Effective," *CNN.com Health,* January 2, 2002, <http://www.cnn.com/2002/HEALTH/01/09/Canadian.cigarettes/> (July 5, 2004).

15. Stanton A. Glantz, "How Many Nonsmokers Does Secondhand Smoke Kill?" *Tobacco.org,* n.d., <http://www.tobacco.org/resources/Health/021022glantz.html> (June 28, 2004).

Chapter 4. Selling a Legal (and Profitable) Drug

1. "Test Your Tobacco IQ," *Joe Chemo,* n.d., <http://www.joechemo.org/cgi-bin/iq.cgi> (February 4, 2004).

2. Ibid.

3. Ibid.

4. J. H. Smiley, "Tobacco," *World Book Online Reference Center,* 2004, <http://www.aolsvc.worldbook.aol.com/wb/Article?id=ar559860> (July 14, 2004).

5. Ibid.

6. Arlene B. Hirschfelder, *Encyclopedia of Smoking and Tobacco* (Phoenix, Ariz.: Oryx Press, 1999), p. 8.

7. Ibid., p. 5.

8. "Test Your Tobacco IQ," *Joe Chemo,* n.d., <http://www.joechemo.org/cgi-bin/iq.cgi> (February 4, 2004).

9. "Find Facts: Money," *Truth,* n.d., <http://www.thetruth.com/index.cfm?seek=facts> (December 14, 2004).

10. Dr. Bob Martin, "The World's Super Power Population Are Killing Themselves!" *Health Talk,* n.d., <http://www.drbobmartin.com/outragearchives.html> (June 19, 2004).

11. Robert Schwebel, *Keep Your Kids Tobacco-Free* (New York: Newmarket Press, 2001), p. 7.

12. William Everett Bailey, *The Invisible Drug* (Houston: Mosaic Publications, 1996), p. 88.

13. American Academy of Pediatrics, "Things You Should Know About Nicotine and Addiction," n.d., <http://www .drbobmartin.com/outragearchives.html> (June 19, 2004).

14. Jimmy Carter, "Tobacco's Big Lie," *The Carter Center,* July 30, 1995, <http://www.cartercenter.org/printdoc.asp?docID =59&submenu=news> (June 25, 2004).

Chapter 5. Winning the Tobacco Wars

1. "Child and Teen Tobacco Use," *American Cancer Society,* Nov. 17, 2003, <http://www.fightcancer.org/ACSWW/ KickTheHabit/TobaccoEffects/ChildTeenTobaccoUse.asp> (July 17, 2004).

2. William Everett Bailey, *The Invisible Drug* (Houston: Mosaic Publications, 1996), p. 83.

3. "Test Your Tobacco IQ," *Joe Chemo,* n.d., <http://www .joechemo.org/cgi-bin/iq.cgi> (February 4, 2004).

4. Drawn from Lawrence Kutner, "Peer Pressure and Smoking," (Philip Morris USA, 2003), p. 8, and Sharon Scott, "Reversing Peer Pressure," *Teen Contact,* n.d., <http://www.teencontact.org/ peer.htm> (June 3, 2004).

5. Barbara S. Lynch and Richard J. Bonnie, eds., *Growing Up Tobacco Free* (Washington, DC: National Academy Press, 1994), p. 41.

6. Ibid, p. 33.

7. "Tips on Quitting," *Joe Chemo,* n.d., <http://www .joechemo.org/cgi-bin/quit.cgi> (February 4, 2004).

8. "About Our Company," *Licensed to Kill, Inc.,* 2003, <http://www.licensedtokill.biz/about.html> (July 19, 2004).

Bailey, William Everett. *The Invisible Drug.* Houston: Mosaic Publications, 1996.

Hirschfelder, Arlene B. *Encyclopedia of Smoking and Tobacco.* Phoenix, Ariz.: Oryx Press, 1999.

Krogh, David. *Smoking: the Artificial Passion.* New York: W. H. Freeman and Co., 1991.

Lang, Susan S. and Beth H. Marks. *Teens & Tobacco: A Fatal Attraction.* New York: Twenty-First Century Books, 1996.

Lynch, Barbara S. and Richard J. Bonnie, eds. *Growing Up Tobacco Free.* Washington, D.C.: National Academy Press, 1994.

McCuen, Gary E. *Tobacco: People, Profits, and Public Health.* Hudson, Wis.: Gem Publications, 1997.

Pringle, Laurence. *Smoking; a Risky Business.* New York: Morrow Junior Books, 1996.

Schwebel, Robert. *Keep Your Kids Tobacco-Free.* New York: Newmarket Press, 2001.

Tate, Cassandra. *Cigarette Wars: the Triumph of "The Little White Slaver."* New York: Oxford University Press, 1999.

Wekesser, Carol, ed. *Smoking.* San Diego, Calif.: Greenhaven Press, 1997.

Phone Numbers to Call for Help

American Cancer Society
1-800-ACS-2345

American Lung Association
1-800-LUNG-USA
1-800-586-4872

Mobilize Against Tobacco for Children's Health
1-800-721-6888

National Network of Tobacco Cessation Quitlines
1-800-QUITNOW
1-800-784-8669